THIS BOOK BELONGS TO:

_____

WELCOME TO GEORGIA

Dedicated to all the travelers out there!

All rights reserved.
No part of this book may be reproduced in any form or by any means, electronic or mechanical, and no photocopying or recording, unless you have written permission from the author.

ISBN 978-1-958985-69-4

Text copyright © 2025 by Mimi Jones

www.joeysavestheday.com

A Mimi Book

Georgia was named after King George II of England, who granted the colony its charter in 1732. The name honored the British monarchy and reflected England's influence over the region. Interestingly, "George" comes from the Greek word georgos, meaning "farmer," a fitting nod to Georgia's agricultural roots.

King Goerge II

ENGLAND

Georgia was the fourth state to join the Union.
It officially joined on January 2, 1788.

Georgia is bordered by the Atlantic Ocean to the east. It shares land borders with five states: Tennessee, North Carolina, South Carolina, Florida, and Alabama.

Atlanta is the capital of Georgia.
It officially became the capital in 1868.

Atlanta, Georgia, has an estimated population of about 510,820 people.

Georgia State Capitol

Georgia is the twenty-second largest state in the U.S., covering 59,425 square miles. It's the biggest state east of the Mississippi River, making it a key part of the Southeast.

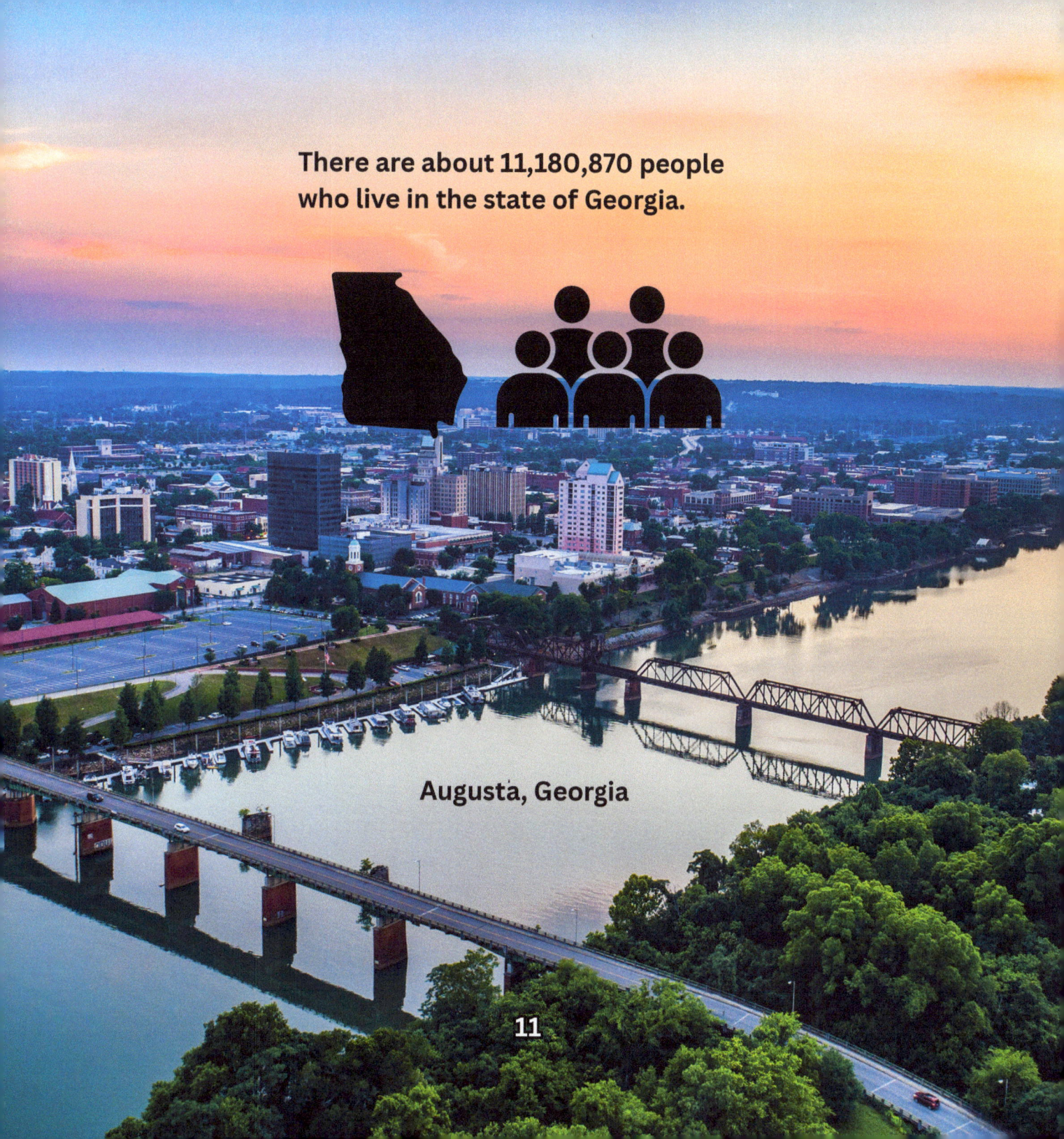

Coca-Cola was invented in 1886 by pharmacist John Stith Pemberton in Atlanta, Georgia. Originally a medicinal tonic, it was first sold at Jacob's Pharmacy, where it was mixed with carbonated water. The name and iconic logo came from Pemberton's bookkeeper, Frank Robinson.

1886

In 1828, the Cherokee Phoenix was established in New Echota, Georgia, becoming the first newspaper published by a Native American tribe.

GEORGIA

There are 159 counties in Georgia.

Here is a list of 20 of them:

Atkinson	Coffee	Hall	Miller	Towns
Bacon	Dade	Jackson	Monroe	Twiggs
Baker	Dodge	Jones	Pickens	Walker
Bulloch	Fayette	Lincoln	Rockdale	Walton
Calhoun	Gilmer	Lumpkin	Sumter	Wilkinson

The Okefenokee Swamp, stretching across 438,000 acres of southeastern Georgia, is the largest blackwater swamp in North America. Its floating peat islands give it an eerie, shifting landscape, and it's home to thousands of alligators and other wildlife.

GEORGIA

Georgia's state tree is the live oak, officially designated on February 25, 1937. This magnificent tree is robust and provides ample shade, making it perfect for a picnic or a cozy nap!

The Savannah River forms part of Georgia's eastern border.

Martin Luther King Jr. was born on January 15, 1929, in Atlanta, Georgia. He grew up to become one of the most important leaders of the Civil Rights Movement. Dr. King believed in creating change through peaceful protest. He spoke out against unfair laws, led marches, and inspired millions with his "I Have a Dream" speech. His work helped our country move toward fairness and equality for everyone.

The brown thrasher is Georgia's state bird. It has reddish-brown feathers and streaks on its chest. Known for its loud and varied songs, it can sing over 1,000 different tunes. First chosen by the governor in 1935, it became the official state bird in 1970 after support from garden clubs across Georgia.

The Vidalia onion is Georgia's most famous vegetable, and for good reason. These onions are grown only in a small region of the state where the soil is low in sulfur, which gives them their distinctive sweet flavor rather than a sharp one. They are named after the town of Vidalia and can only be cultivated in a few surrounding counties, such as Toombs and Tattnall.

The Cherokee rose, with its soft white petals and golden heart, became Georgia's state flower on August 18, 1916. Chosen for its beauty and symbolism, this climbing bloom carries a deeper meaning rooted in sorrow and strength. According to legend, during the Trail of Tears, Cherokee mothers wept as they were forced from their land. Where their tears touched the earth, the Cherokee rose is said to have bloomed.

Georgia is often referred to as "The Goober State" due to its significant peanut production. This plays a significant role in its agricultural economy. It is also informally known as "The Empire State of the South," reflecting its historical significance and economic influence in the southern United States.

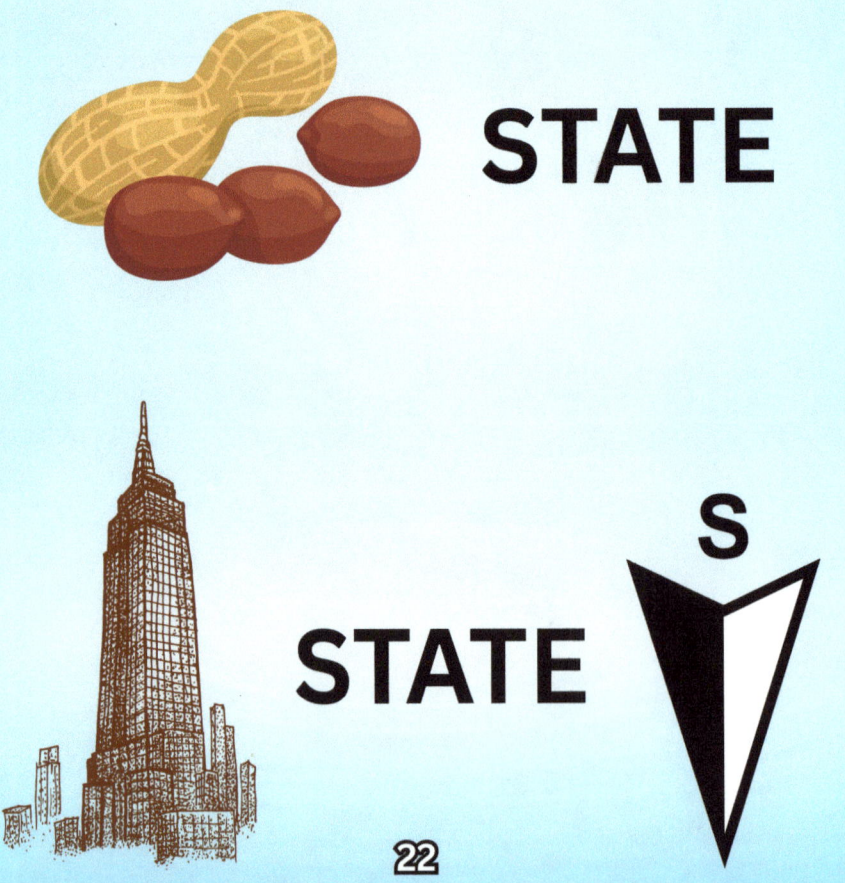

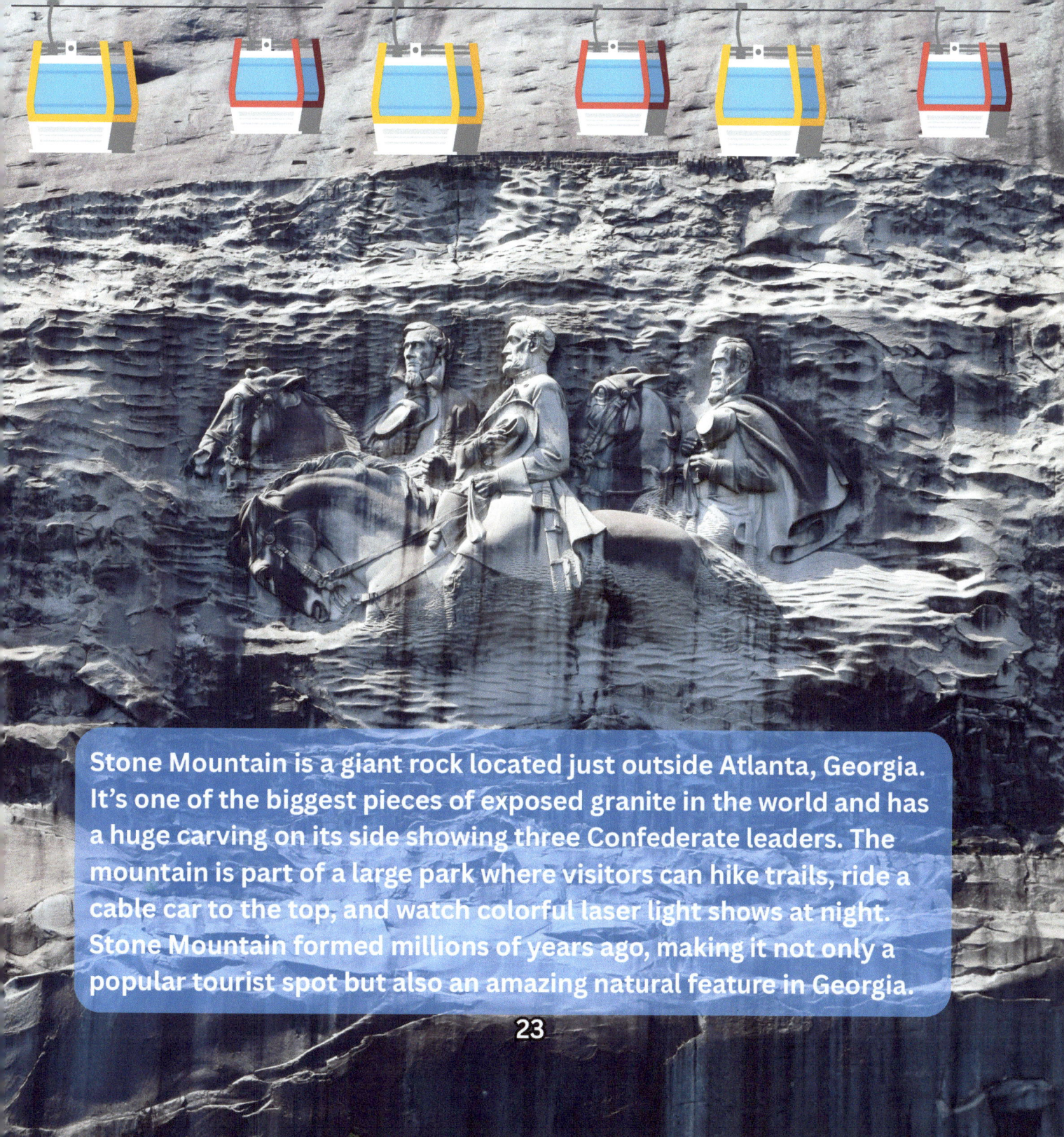

Stone Mountain is a giant rock located just outside Atlanta, Georgia. It's one of the biggest pieces of exposed granite in the world and has a huge carving on its side showing three Confederate leaders. The mountain is part of a large park where visitors can hike trails, ride a cable car to the top, and watch colorful laser light shows at night. Stone Mountain formed millions of years ago, making it not only a popular tourist spot but also an amazing natural feature in Georgia.

GEORGIA
GEORGIA
GEORGIA

The abbreviation for Georgia is GA.

GA

Georgia's first official flag was adopted on October 17, 1879. However, there is a possibility that an earlier version may have existed prior to this date, although details about it remain unclear. The flag that represents Georgia today was officially designated as the state flag on May 8, 2003.

Some of the crops grown in Georgia are blueberries, corn, cotton, hay, peaches, and peanuts.

Some of the animals that live in Georgia include alligators, armadillos, chipmunks, foxes, and white-tailed deer.

Georgia exhibits significant temperature fluctuations throughout the year. The state recorded its highest temperature at 112 degrees Fahrenheit in Louisville on July 24, 1952. In contrast, the lowest temperature documented in Georgia was -17 degrees Fahrenheit (17 degrees below zero) on January 27, 1940.

Jimmy Carter was born on October 1, 1924, in the small town of Plains, Georgia. He grew up on a peanut farm. Carter later became the 39th President of the United States, known for his focus on peace, fairness, and helping people around the world.

Moderation

Georgia's official state motto is "Wisdom, Justice, and Moderation," which encapsulates the values the state aims to uphold.

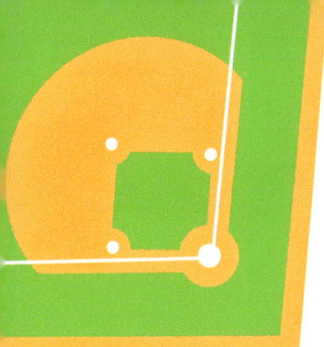  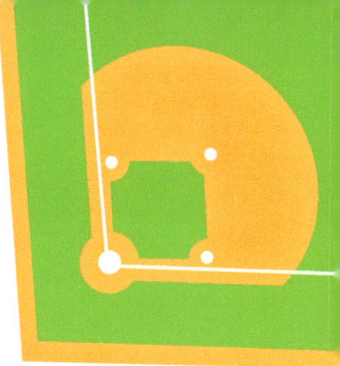

The Atlanta Braves are Georgia's very own Major League Baseball team! Based in Cumberland, just outside Atlanta, the Braves have a long and exciting history, with their most recent World Series win in 2021. They play at a beautiful stadium called Truist Park.

Georgia's NFL team is the Atlanta Falcons! They're the only NFL team based in the state and play their home games at Mercedes-Benz Stadium in downtown Atlanta. The Falcons joined the league in 1966 and have built a passionate fan base known for their loud cheers and signature "Rise Up" chant.

WAR

The Battle of Atlanta was a significant and pivotal battle during the American Civil War, which took place on July 22, 1864. Union General William T. Sherman wanted to capture Atlanta because it was a major railroad and supply center for the South. Ultimately, the Union army emerged victorious. This victory gave a significant boost to the North and helped President Abraham Lincoln secure re-election.

Near the city of Savannah, you'll find Georgia's oldest and tallest lighthouse! It was first built way back in 1736 and has been rebuilt a few times since. Today, it stands 144 feet high, and brave visitors can climb 178 steps to reach the top for an amazing view of the ocean.

Can you name these?

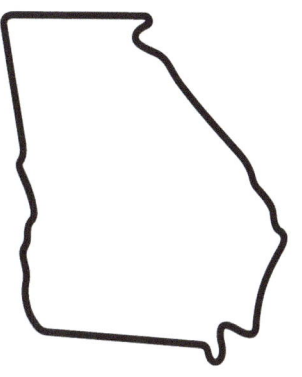 

I hope you enjoyed
learning about
Georgia.

To explore fun facts about the other 49 states, visit my website at www.joeysavestheday.com. You'll also find a wide variety of homeschool resources to support joyful learning at home. If you enjoyed this book, I would be grateful if you left a review. Your feedback truly helps. Thank you for your support!

Check out these other interesting books in the
50 States Fact Books Series!

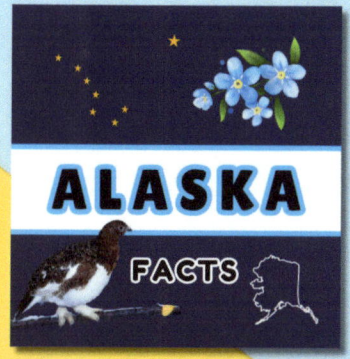

www.mimibooks.com

www.ingramcontent.com/pod-product-compliance
Lightning Source LLC
Chambersburg PA
CBHW040027050426
42453CB00002B/34